Will We See Animals?

by Megan Litwin

Editorial Offices: Glenview, Illinois • Parsippany, New Jersey • New York, New York
Sales Offices: Needham, Massachusetts • Duluth, Georgia • Glenview, Illinois
Coppell, Texas • Sacramento, California • Mesa, Arizona

We hike into the woods.

Many animals live here.

Which animals will we see?

We can see birds.

They live in a nest.

They are at home in the woods.

We can see a fox.

It can hunt in the snow.

It is at home in the woods.

We can see an ant.

It looks for its nest.

It is at home in the woods.

What a good hike in the woods!
We saw many animals at home
in the woods.
You can see them too!

Ants

As we saw in the book, many different animals make their homes in the woods. Ants are one kind of woods animal. Ants live in nests that have many rooms and tunnels. The nests have one or more queen ants and lots of worker ants. The queen ant is the mother of all the ants in the nest. The worker ants take care of ant eggs and feed baby ants.